All I needed to know about projects, I learned as a kid shoveling snow

Earning a motorcycle

PETE THOMPSON

WestBow
PRESS
A DIVISION OF THOMAS NELSON

WestBow Press books may be ordered
through booksellers or by contacting:

WestBow Press
A Division of Thomas Nelson
1663 Liberty Drive
Bloomington, IN 47403
www.westbowpress.com
1-(866) 928-1240

ISBN: 978-1-4497-3047-5 (sc)
ISBN: 978-1-4497-3046-8 (e)

Library of Congress Control Number: 2011919651

Printed in the United States of America

WestBow Press rev. date: 11/10/2011

Dedication

For my mother and father. Their steadfast decisions taught me that I may not always be given what I want, but I can always work towards obtaining whatever I desire.

Epigraph

You'll shoot your eye out.[1]

---

[1] *A Christmas Story.* Dir. Bob Clark. Perf. Peter Billingsley, Melinda Dillon and Darren McGavin. 1983. Film

Table of Contents

Forward

'The eternal story: youthful dreams, undismayed by reality, followed by Herculean efforts to achieve the dreams, followed by . . . . reality.

> Barry Flachsbart, Professor IST, Missouri University of Science & Technology

Preface

In Business 101, the professor liked to say, "There are no problems in business, only opportunities." I used to think it was some happy hogwash overenthusiastic and naive business majors regurgitated to sound like "innovative go getters." It may very well be just a cliche for some, but by the end of the semester I grokked what the professor meant; look at problems as business opportunities.

The following pages tell my story as a 12 year old discovering the fundamentals of virtually any project, a little business, and some customer relationship management. This aspect of my education took place when I was shoveling snow, trying to earn enough money to buy a motorcycle.

Thanks to the editors, Mrs. Bloomington and Dr. Flachsbart and especially my childhood friend and business partner, Mel R. Yenchak.

The idea

He walked along the dirt trail with his gaze a few feet ahead—taking stock of loose, unstable rocks and fallen or low hanging tree branches. He was envisioning himself riding a motorcycle and contemplating the split second decisions to route the fastest possible path. But all he could do was imagine and try to relate what his friends had told him about their riding excitement. Pete had never ridden a motorcycle, although he had occasionally ridden Mel's ATC.

He didn't really like the 3-wheeler because it seemed awkward and he had this fear of running over himself if a foot slipped off a peg. This almost happened once when he panicked and put his foot down to thwart a potential tip. He didn't get pulled under the machine but got a painful ankle sprain when the back tire hit his heel. This instability is why his Mom thought ATC's were "so dangerous." Four-wheelers were more stable and "safer" from the tipping point of view, but the added weight was a crushing blow in the eyes of a Mom. Anyway, his friends thought 4-wheelers were lame and they were more expensive than 3-wheelers which complicated the situation further.

At this point he was getting desperate. He just wanted some sort of dirt bike so he could participate in the excitement his friends talked about while pointing to pictures in magazines and narrating the scene's action as if they were part of it. He envied them and all the fun he missed out on because his parents would not buy him either a two, three, or four-wheeled off-road vehicle.

Just like the protagonist in *A Christmas Story* hinting his Red Ryder BB gun Christmas gift wishes to his parents, Pete followed suit the previous year with a 4-wheeler. Pete left magazines turned to specific pages in conspicuous places and even slid motorcycle ads into his parent's literature just like Ralphie promoting his dream of "old blue." When Santa didn't bring Pete a Honda 200 SX 4-wheeler, he kept waiting for his Dad to remember the key—like Ralphie's Dad just happened to see the unopened present behind the tree. Unlike Ralphie, the Honda 200 SX 4-wheeler would remain a dream.

As he continued up the hill, walking his imaginary motorized route around boulders and gullies, it occurred to him. The only strategy he had not attempted was asking for permission to buy a motorcycle with his own money. The saving was fairly easy, the tricky part was earning it.

The pitch

On the ride home, Pete pitched the idea. "If I can save enough money for a motorcycle, will you allow me to purchase one with my earnings?"

Mom responded immediately with "NOOOO! You are not getting a 3-wheeler!"

"What about a 4-wheeler or motorcycle?" Pete fired back.

"It's not that we don't want to buy you one . . . where are you going to ride it?" His Dad questioned.

"In the woods behind the house." Pete confidently replied. There was a 1/4 acre of woods behind the house and Pete had already mapped a trail in his head.

"There's not enough room!" His Mom interjected. She had a point . . . the path was quite serpentine to avoid obstacles such as fallen trees or large rocks.

"There is plenty of room, just not enough to go fast." Pete replied (realizing this was a major selling point!). Somehow he had to squelch his Mom's image of Evil Knievel's body cartwheeling through the air after failing a jump. "It's not like I'll be jumping cars or anything."

"You'll get bored." His Dad said.

"So I can jump cars then?!" Pete replied with his wise-ass tone—quickly feeling his father's annoyed glare from the rearview mirror.

"Well, what about the neighbors?!" Mom shouted back. "I don't think they want to live next to a motorcycle dirt track!" It was always about the neighbors.

"Pete, we've had this discussion before. I am not buying you a motorcycle!" Dad commanded. But this discussion was different. Pete wasn't asking his parents to buy him a motorcycle; he was asking for *permission* to buy a motorcycle.

"I know you aren't going to buy me one!" Pete said, "If I can save enough money to buy one; promise to ride it only in the woods and not on the lawn or roads; get approval from the neighbors and always wear a helmet, may I *please* buy a motorcycle?"

The silence was deafening. After what seemed like an eternity, his Dad replied, "Sure!"

His mother looked at his father in shock, as did Pete. Confirming the decision, she asked "You are going to let him buy a motorcycle?"

His father obviously tired of Pete's pestering—and expecting to end the discussion conclusively replied, "If he wants to waste his own money on a motorcycle, that's fine with me!"

"Well . . ." she stammered, "you are going to have to get a helmet! What about gas? Where are you going to put it?" It seemed like her list of complications was endless, but it didn't matter. With one word, "Sure" in the context of motorcycle ownership, he gave Pete permission, to buy a one. All he had to do now was earn the money.

The beginning

There had been an early frost that year. The grass stopped growing for the season and the trees had shed their leaves. Now Pete had a valid reason to earn and save money, but there were no lawns to mow and he refused to rake leaves! Around that time, there was an unseasonable early snow fall, a light dusting by east coast standards, only an inch or so. Pete had to shovel his driveway before he was allowed to go sledding, but the snow on the street wasn't thick enough to sled on anyway. When his family lived in Indiana the garage was behind the house and not attached—making for a very long driveway. To save time, his father had purchased a shovel about three feet wide that would clear the narrow and longest stretch of the drive in three or four overlapping passes. Pete thought that was the coolest thing and couldn't wait until he was old enough, big enough really, to use it. On end, the shovel was taller than Pete and must have weighed 25 pounds! One day, when he was a big boy, he'd be able to use it Dad promised. Pete was bigger, twelve years old now, tall for his age but was he big enough to employ the big boy shovel? One way to find out. When he tried to pick it up the varnished wood slid through his gloved grip. He bent down and grasped the thicker, less handled section of the shaft closer to the business end of the tool. Ugh! It was heavy, but once on the drive, all he had to do was push it. The tarred blacktop surface was quite slick when covered with snow. It's difficult to determine if it was anxious anticipation for having the opportunity to use the big boy shovel or fatigue from uncovering then transporting the behemoth to the garage opening, but once there he released his grip allowing the blade to practically free-fall to the ground. Being almost three feet wide, an uneven landing was inevitable even from six inches. One end hit before the other with a loud thud-clang that jolted the wooden handle from his grip and struck his cheek. After a casual glance to see if he had to play it off as if "he meant to do it," he grabbed the close to the cheek end with his right hand, exerted downward force mid-shaft with his left hand and began to push. The blade stayed put but his hands slid down the polished handle as if it were greased. He let go of the shovel and the handle struck the asphalt surface with a reverberating dong as he jumped over the blade to dispel the forward momentum and regain his balance. Again, he casually surveyed the scene to see if any audience members witnessed his latest trick. Luckily, the theater was empty. This time he picked up the very end of the shovel shaft and placed it on the heel of his right hand, cocked his elbow and brought his wrist in to his chest. "This time, there will be no slip ups, he had a good grip on the situation" he mused to himself. His right hand was taking all the pressure forcing the shovel to move forward. In this configuration, his left hand could do nothing more than keep the end of the shaft from falling out of his right which was unfortunate because he is a southpaw.

He began his descent at the widest part of the drive and this handling procedure was much more effective. With each step, the shovel became a little bit heavier with all the snow building up in front of it, but he was still going strong. About a quarter of the way, the building snow pile began falling over the top of the blade and after a few more steps became very difficult to push. Pete stopped and began to transfer small piles of snow from the drive to the grass until his big pile was gone. This routine continued at approximately the fifty and seventy-five percent lengths of the drive as well and Pete was getting fatigued. He believed that the open space would allow him to apply more body language to increase leverage on the monster tool—which it did—but the additional freedom did little for decreasing the chore of lifting the remaining snow off the drive. For the last leg, he realized he could just push the snow into the street! He started his way back up the drive but only made it about fifteen percent before it became too difficult to push. So, he decided to use the shoveled path as a starting place to push the snow to the grass widthwise. Although it seemed like he had to pick the heavy shovel up more often, it was much cleaner than the long run. With each pass, he got closer to the section which widens out to a two car width. Although this meant he was getting closer to being finished, it also meant he was going to have longer stretches to push, resulting in bigger piles to relocate. He felt confident that he could push the snow to the edge, then scoop smaller amounts he could lift with the monstrous shovel and carry it to the grass. That's what he did, well sort of. By now Pete was exhausted and he did not make it as far as he expected to and the idea of carrying smaller loads of snow and that huge shovel back and forth from the pile to the grass appeared to be an ominous and overwhelming task. It was time to use the regular all purpose 18" snow shovel. It had an actual plastic handle at the end of the shaft which he grabbed with his left hand and he chuckled at how light this shovel was. He was able to scoop a full load and toss it to the edge from where he was standing, making short work of the remaining pile. He continued this run with the regular shovel. Although it required more scooping and tossing actions, they required much less effort than the big boy shovel. Pete continued shoveling the rest of the drive with the smaller shovel. On his trip back to the garage he noticed the big boy shovel laying in the middle of the snow cleaned drive. He put the smaller one away then went to retrieve the big boy. Pete was somewhat proud of himself for putting the monster shovel to use and also had a better understanding of why it did not get much use. The cliches, "right tool for the job" and "work smarter, not harder" crossed his mind.

The team

A few weeks went by before the next snowfall. After he finished his drive with the 18" shovel, Pete decided to try to drum up a little business and ask his neighbors if he may shovel their drives. The family across the street had a son Pete's age and they always shoveled their own. The families on either side of them, hired a company to plow theirs as did the grouchy older couple on the north side of Pete's house. The house to the south was empty and for sale and the realtor only had it plowed if she had a showing. Other families on his street had kids Pete's age or older to shovel their drives and it wasn't worth asking.

Pete's mom always made him shovel the walkway to the front door which was a pain and nobody used it. The steps were originally constructed with slate slabs laying on top of loose bricks, creating a very unstable, uneven and inconsistent staircase. Even during the summer months walking them was risky, and with a little snow and ice you were almost guaranteed to slip and fall, even wearing boots with good tread. If his parents were expecting company, Pete would get the job of watching for them to arrive then let them in through the garage so they could walk up the basement stairs instead. Most of the front walkways around the neighborhood were built as decorative footpaths with complete disregard to Blondel's ergonomic formula for tread and riser dimensions, and not for actual use. He noticed the plowing companies did not shovel walkways. In all likelihood for this very reason, they were not used. The driveway layouts always had one section that was un-plowable and most drivers would not leave the warm driver's seat to shovel that either, and yet these companies commanded $25-$30 per house. Of course, the companies would have your driveway plowed in less than 10 minutes and could be hired for the season. So the convenience and consistency was worth the cost. As long as people could get in and out of their garages, the small un-plowed patch was considered acceptable. It also gave the husband the opportunity to be a man and "finish the job" by clearing off the small un-plowed section of the drive himself.

Realizing there was a slim chance of finding a drive to shovel near by, Pete decided to go to a friend's house instead. When he arrived, Mel was finishing his drive but still had to do the dreaded walkway to the front door. Pete being the impatient chap that he was, grabbed a shovel from the garage and started shoveling it with him. When they were both done, Mel said he had to shovel his neighbor's drive for $20. At first Pete as a little irritated, since the only reason he helped Mel with his drive was so that they could do something else. But then Pete seized the opportunity and said he'd help Mel if he split the money with him. After a moment's hesitation, Mel agreed. It was amazing how much faster and easier it seemed when two people were sharing the job. When they finished that drive, Pete suggested they shovel another. Mel agreed. A partnership was born.

The customer

At the first house, Ms. Strickland's, while waiting for an answer, Mel started shoveling off the front steps. Pete said, "What are you doing that for? They haven't paid us yet!"

Mel shrugged his shoulders and said, "I don't know."

When Ms. Strickland answered the door she looked at the stoop and noticed that it had been shoveled. Since they were both holding shovels, the first thing she said in a rhetorical tone was "Did you guys do that? Thank you!" Before they could get a word out, she continued with "I guess you are here to shovel my drive! Or did you do that too and now you want your money?"

Without missing a beat, Mel replied, "Yup! Twenty bucks!"

In a scolding almost frantic tone she replied with, "Well I'm not paying. I have the lawn service under contract. Not very smart business boys. You can't just ask people to pay for a service they didn't request!"

Pete just stood there in shock when Mel said, "OK, we'll put it back."

She paused for a moment with a look of horror on her face until she realized Mel was joking and started laughing. She said "I'm sorry boys, but I'm already committed."

Mel replied, "That's OK, we understand."

As they were walking toward the next house, they heard Ms. Strickland's door open and she started yelling, "Boys!? Boys!? Wait!" Mel and Pete exchanged glances wondering what now? "Come back! I changed my mind! You can shovel my drive!"

Pete jokingly said to Mel, "It looks like we're both gonna make $20 on this drive since our price just doubled!"

When they turned around and were walking toward Ms. Strickland's door, she shouted across the yard, "I just called the lawn service and they aren't plowing drives this year. How much do you boys charge?"

Simultaneously Mel said "twenty" and Pete said "thirty."

She said, "You boys need to get your story straight. How about twenty-five?"

They looked at each other and said, "OK!"

As they were walking to the drive, Pete said to Mel, "Damn-it! I knew I should've said forty! Maybe she will only have two twenties, and gee, we don't have change!"

Mel said, "Nah, I'll bet she writes a check."

Sure enough, she already had the check written before they even finished the lot . . . except for the "payable to:" line. She asked "This is my last check. Who do you want it made out to."

Mel gave her *his* name.

She said, "Oh, you are Alice's boy! I thought you looked familiar! How's the family?" Mel assured her they were all doing well. She tore the check out of the book and handed it to him.

Pete was fuming—concerned that he'd never get his money from Mel. Here shoveling drives was Pete's idea, and now Mel was taking all bounty!

Ms. Strickland shared that a few of the neighbors had the same lawn service and suggested talking to them about shoveling too.

This cheered Pete up a little, because they could just alternate collection. But he still felt the extra five should go to him. Of course, then again, it was Mel's shovel Pete was using and Mel's neighbor that gave them the leads which resulted in two more drives at twenty per drive that night. So Mel now owed Pete thirty-seven fifty. Pete let Mel slide on the two fifty because he felt it was a small price to pay for access to Mel's tools and his mom's social network.

The pickup

A couple times a year, the township would allow homeowners to discard larger items such as furniture and other basement or garage clutter. Pete and his friends would ride their BMX bicycles and survey the trash for anything they could make a ramp out of or an item to jump over. This year, there was a small electric snow blower Mel took particular interest in, and he stopped to investigate. His father was a mechanic and his mother taught grade school art, so this made Mel mechanically artistic in his approach to problem solving and a natural born tinkerer. Unfortunately the cliche, "We mock what we don't understand" applied to Mel, and he took the brunt of many jokes. Luckily he was good natured with a genuinely likable character because with his Scandinavian heritage, he was the biggest and strongest kid throughout the school years. Most people didn't pick on him to be mean, but because they could get away with it. Sometimes he would say or do things that would make people just say, "Duh!" But remember the cliche? His rationale was generally plausible, but they mocked him because it seemed only Mel understood his approach.

A few days later there was another snow storm. This time it was three inches of a wet snow . . . the kind that is good for making snowballs to be thrown because it sticks together. The same holds true when shoveling. The snow can be accurately tossed greater distances than powder. The effort to time relationship is a fascinating conundrum. Since the shovelfuls can be tossed farther, it appears easier to go faster with only a small increase in effort. One full driveway, no problem, but add two albeit cooperative driveways, and you have exhaustion! Walking down Mel's drive to his garage, they were discussing how tired they were—and although considerably colder, how much easier it was the last time to shovel powder. Mel opened the garage door and there it was, almost as if it were intentionally placed there by the work gods and the 80 watt incandescent bulb focused like a spotlight in a theater and angels sang, the electric snow blower that Pete and pals so ruthlessly ridiculed Mel for absconding with. Again, the Mel Rationale triumphed. The next time it snowed, they had a power tool!

The labor saving device

In a couple days, they were blanketed with six inches of powder. When they went to the first house, Ms. Strickland's, there were fresh tire tracks in the snow and they assumed she was not home. The snow might have been light and fluffy but it was still difficult to walk in, so they left the machine by the street in case she was not home. As it turned out, she had just gotten home from the night before. She answered the door obviously exhausted from being up all night. "Good timing! I was on my way to bed. It's been a long night! Go ahead and shovel. I'll leave a check taped to the door!" She belted as the door slammed shut.

Mel shrugged his shoulders and Pete said, "OK."

He started on the walkway while Mel walked out to the street to get the machine. Pete heard the front door open. He turned to see the homeowner taping an envelope to the front door. In a sarcastic tone she yelled, "Where's Mel going? He forget a shovel?"

Before Pete had a chance to respond, the door slammed shut again. The walkway was finished by the time Mel got the machine going—which seemed a little odd since it was electric. As it turned out, he couldn't find an outlet with power so he used Ms. Strickland's neighbors. Pete decided to shovel the end of the drive since the electric snow blower would be useless on this densely packed mess the street plow provided them with. He was also getting a little irritated because he was doing all the hard physical labor while Mel was screwing around with the machine! The whole idea behind using the snow blower was to decrease effort and time, but thus far it had only increased time and Pete's share of the workload. So Pete decided to only shovel half of the end of the drive. Pete, feeling smug about his decision to let Mel do the rest of the drive, sat down in the snow to wait for him.

Shortly thereafter, he heard the whining of the electric motor as Mel approached. Then it stopped. Mel yelled, "What are you doing?"

Pete shouted back "Waiting for you to finish."

Mel countered, "This thing can't handle that!"

Pete said, "I know." While lifting up his shovel, suggesting Mel would have to shovel it.

Mel replied "Duh! Just do it!" as he started the snow blower and headed towards the garage.

Pete was feeling kind of lazy and figured he was not earning his share of the take even though Mel had the "easy part." Besides, the quicker they finish this drive, the quicker they could move to the next one. Pete was reluctantly preparing to work on Mel's half—hoping Mel would finish before he did when there was an odd thud and the electric whine of the machine stopped. Pete mentally accused Mel of stalling to shirk responsibility of the real work, but Pete didn't say anything and finished the end of the drive as Mel was doing something with the machine. On the last shovel, Pete proclaimed "OK! I'm done! You can quit screwing around!"

Mel replied with a disgusted, "I hit the newspaper!"

Pete laughed and said, "What did you do that for?! Throw her in reverse!" Knowing full well it did not have reverse, but Mel looked anyway.

They were amazed at how such a simple thing could cause such a difficult problem. Part of the paper made its way into the chute and part was pinned between the blade and the housing—rendering it inaccessible with gloved or bare hands. If the machine did have reverse, the paper would've popped right out mostly intact, but the blade would only rotate one way, apparently by design which in hindsight seems dangerous, especially since they had their hands in there. The only options were to force it forward destroying the paper and possibly the machine . . . or give up. At this point, the dilemma became a challenge to the ingenuity of their preteen manhood. Using the shovel handle as a pry bar, they were able to apply enough force on the blade to cut the paper in two. Half fell out the bottom and the other was easily removed from the chute. Once powered-on, the machine worked fine. As Mel finished the rest of the drive, Pete went to get their money. There was an envelope taped to the door with Mel's name on it. In the envelope was a check for nineteen dollars and a handwritten note which read. "I subtracted $5 because I am paying you boys to 'shovel' my drive for the effort and money relationship lesson it teaches. Using the snow blower is a good application of work smarter, not harder but at the expense of quality because the drive is cleaner when you boys use shovels. The extra dollar was subtracted to cover the newspaper destroyed by your snow blower." This drive shouldn't have taken them more than 15 minutes, yet they had been there for two and a half hours! Instead of reducing time, it increased . . . while reducing their take. Pete was not pleased and tempted to just give up for the day when he got the bright idea to guilt Mel into letting him use the snow blower at the next house while Mel shoveled the walk and worked on the end of the drive. After some bickering, Mel agreed.

The technique

On the way to the front door, they looked over the drive to try to determine if a paper was buried beneath the snow. Luckily, they found it on the lawn not far from the stoop. When a homeowner answers the door and the winter cold rips through their pajamas to the warm skin underneath, the unpleasant thought of going outside to shovel becomes a reality. Here they thought they were going to have to get dressed and hunt through the snow for the newspaper and figure while they were out there, they might as well shovel. Handing the paper to the person who answered the door was a fantastic deal closer when combined with shoveling the front steps. It almost seemed like they feel obligated, which sometimes bothered Pete, but that guilty feeling was often smothered by those who said they were grateful for them bringing the papers and shoveling the stairs but did not want them to shovel the drive. Usually it was because they had a service, but now, Mel and Pete were that service the homeowners depended on.

Pete thought using the snow blower would be a breeze, but it blow-ed, pun intended. The wheels did not roll very well caked with snow and ice and when the wheels did turn the left did so more freely than the right. Not only did this make it difficult to push but took some effort to aim. The chute did not rotate freely when using the aluminum control rod which had the tendency to flex when repositioning the chute that moved from the vibrations. To move forward in a straight line and get the blown snow to land in the grass the operator had to push with the right arm while pulling with the left. This took its toll on Pete's arms on the first pass down the drive. The method with the most consistent results involved pushing the bar-handle with his stomach and right arm, then pulling the bar to his stomach with his left arm to keep it straight. To make things worse, with his body positioned like that, it was difficult for him to get traction. There had to be a trick that Mel didn't tell him about, but Pete was afraid to ask because he didn't want to look like an idiot, or end up with Mel taking over since Pete was "incapable." On the next pass Pete decided to knock some of the snow off the blower by quickly rocking it from left to right, essentially slamming it from wheel to wheel. If the impact was too hard the blade would strike the housing with an eerie grinding sound. On the bright side, the harder the impact the more ice and snow that was dislodged. Mel yelled at Pete telling him to stop, so Pete did it a couple more times out of spite.

The machine was more controllable for maybe half of the drive length, then the snow and ice began building up with the aforementioned issues recurring. No problem, Pete had the rockin' strategy. Over confident in his machine cleaning scheme, Pete figured Mel could do cleanup after finishing the walk. Pete rocked, caked snow and ice fell, all was good in the hood. Like before the machine worked well for about half of the drive, then became increasing troublesome the closer the end became. Pete had two more passes and a combination of the vibration, and nuances of device control had taken their toll on him. Due to fatigue, the rockin' results were less effective and he was less able to control the machine as the snow built up again. By the time Pete finished his last pass, Mel had finished cleaning up after him. When Pete powered off the machine his arms were tingling from the vibrations. Mel asked "so how was it?". Pete replied, "It was OK. What do you say we switch off?" Mel agreed. Pete had absolutely no desire to use the machine anymore because he felt it was too difficult to use and didn't think it did a very good job anyway. Mel went to the door to collect the check as Pete collected the power cord.

At the next house, Mel seemed to get the knack for operating the machine, which Pete was happy about. There was still some cleanup but finally the contraption seemed to do what it was supposed to do. As previously mentioned, many of the walkways were only for show and the homeowners did not expect it to be as clean as the drive. This meant Pete could start working on cleanup and the plow pile at the street. They ended up doing six drives that day. The next week two storms rolled through separated by a day and they were able to knock out six drives each day at $20 a house.

The service

The following Monday Pete was running a fever and his mom kept him home from school on Tuesday. As luck would have it, another storm rolled through and school was cancelled on Wednesday. Since Pete stayed home the day before, he was not allowed to leave the house—not even to shovel his own drive (which was fine since Pete felt crappy even though the fever had broken Tuesday morning). Pete was a little nervous and to a certain extent jealous that Mel could clear the regular customers' drives by himself with the aid of the machine. If he could do it himself, why split the money with Pete? As it turned out, Mel only cleared his drive.

The following week, the tables turned, and this time Mel was sick. When Pete called, Mel's mother answered the phone and would not let him talk to Mel because he was asleep. So Pete waited an hour and called again, but Mel was still asleep. Pete was quite irritated because for some reason he believed he had a "right" to use the snow blower, but was taught to ask for permission. Feeling smug, he called back to request consent. Mel's mother informed Pete that Dustin, Mel's older brother, was using the machine to clear their drive and when he finished had to clear Ms. Strickland's drive. Mel's Mom said Ms. Strickland had called to see if "Mel and that other boy were 'working' today." Apparently she was very angry that Mel and Pete did not show up the previous week to shovel. She had become accustomed to their service. Pete told Mel's Mom that he would go to Ms. Strickland's and shovel for her. The last thing he wanted was to lose a customer, especially to Mel's older brother. She seemed shocked that Pete was going to ride his bicycle all the way down there just to shovel a driveway and tried to talk him out of it. Pete persisted and eventually she agreed to tell Dustin not to go to Ms. Strickland's but suggested Pete bring a shovel, which seemed odd because Pete always used one of Mel's shovels and the snow blower.

Half of the way there, Pete was beginning to question his "dedication." Mel's Mom told

Pete the streets had not been plowed but he thought he could just ride in the vehicle tire tracks which he usually did . . . when not carrying a shovel. The shovel made it awkward to pedal and to compensate had to over steer, sometimes out of the packed tire track which would throw off his balance. He was concerned that if it took him too long, Dustin would go to Ms. Strickland's to do Pete's job. A few houses from Mel's, Pete heard the idle of a 4-stroke engine. Then it became constant and, shortly thereafter, he saw a headlight approaching. It looked like there were two people on a three-wheeler and they were pulling something. It was Darrell with Dustin on the back towing a sled carrying two shovels and Mel's snow blower! They were laughing at Pete as they whizzed by. He could hear the tools shifting on the plastic sled as it bounced into a groove. The whole reason he agreed to shovel Ms. Strickland's drive was because he planned on using the snow blower!

The procrastinate

When he got to Ms. Strickland's, he tossed his bike on to the snow next to the mailbox and started shoveling at the street since the plows had not been by—although there was still a fair amount of buildup from the previous snow! He had to shovel essentially two snowfalls, by himself, for the price of one. It was unseasonably warm the day after the previous storm. Luckily, this worked to Pete's advantage as the previous snow created an ice sheet so both snowfalls were removed at once, and when it did, the driveway was uncovered almost perfectly clean and dry. As with wet snow, ice is heavier, but not toss-able like wet snow since the stiff sheet had the tendency to slide off the shovel which took a little extra time and effort to balance. Now all that was left were the two, one-foot tire tracks from Ms. Strickland's Jeep.

Pete did not make the connection, but he was using the edge between the tire packed and unpacked snow to get underneath the previous snow. Sometimes it was easy to get an edge and the track peeled up. Other times the shovel slipped, further smoothing the already icy edge—making it impossible to get underneath it. He tried kicking it with his heel which had some effect, but it was difficult to keep his balance. So then he tried the corner of the shovel, which chopped right through, the first time—rounding the corner so naturally Pete tried the other corner and rounded it, too. Then he tried the leading edge of the shovel which would've worked perfectly had the metal been stronger, but the curved blade just absorbed by the impact. All that was left was the handle end of the shovel—which broke apart the track with no problem—although it required many strikes since the impact zone was about the size of a dime. Rather than keep switching from end to end, Pete decided to just go down the line breaking the ice with the end and then go back and remove it with the shovel. That worked great for about ten feet until his arms got tired; then he'd go back to shovel the broken ice where he left off chopping. As Pete was finishing the left track, he accidentally put the shovel down curved side up which created a more blunt edge which was easier than striking and also peeled the packed track. Pete was eager to put this new technique to use on the right track which was literally hit or miss. Using all three techniques, the right track was a lot easier. As it turned out, the snow blower would have been useless. Now to the walkway!

The conversation

Without the edge, he didn't know how he was going to get down to the surface. The only thing he was accomplishing was uncovering the previous snowfall. Completely exhausted, parched, and hungry, the garage door opened and Ms. Strickland backed out her Jeep. Pete stopped trying to get the walk started and stood on the snow covered lawn as she pulled up even with him. She rolled down the window and said, "That's OK. No one uses it anyway."

Pete's dread was replaced with delight.

Before he could say, "Thank you," she asked, "Where do you live?"

Pete replied, "On Lampshade."

She said, "You came a long way just to shovel my drive! I'll make you a deal. If you get today's newspaper, I'll give you a lift home."

As she began rolling up her window, Pete replied, "Deal!"

The delivery boy tossed the paper not far from Pete's bike while he was shoveling. When he returned to the Jeep with the paper and his bike, she cracked the window and shouted, "Trunks open!"

Pete popped the trunk and could feel the heat pouring from the interior.

"I put a towel down, but shake your bike off." She shouted.

Pete did just that. Due to the bouncy nature of bicycle tires, very little snow fell off and the bike almost slammed into the car. He was so tired, it was difficult to lift the bike into the trunk far enough for the door to close without sliding it on the towel. So it was half on, half off. When he was trying to lift the front wheel to pull the towel underneath, she shouted, "Hurry up! I'm cold!" Pete hastily knocked the snow off the shovel and placed it next to his bike and closed the door.

When he opened the passenger side door, Ms. Strickland's hand shot out and she barked, "Where's my paper?!" Pete brushed the snow from the blue bag protecting the paper, and handed it to her.

"What about last weeks?" She said with a contemptuous tone.

Pete retorted, "You only asked for today's!"

She chuckled and said, "You're right! Hop in! I hope there wasn't anything newsworthy! I won't see that paper for another few months. Shake the snow off your boots before you get in!"

"It's a Jeep! Why do you care?!" Pete thought to himself. His legs were so tired he could barely raise his boots to tap them against the door jam, but he did as he was told.

"Although we've been doing business for a few weeks now, I don't believe we've met. I'm Margaret Strickland. Who are you?"

"I'm Pete" he said.

"Nice to meet you, Pete." She said with her right hand extended to shake. "Do you have a last name?"

Pete shook her hand and said, "Thompson. Pete Thompson."

She grinned and said, "Well, buckle-up, Pete Thompson. Where on Lampshade are we going?"

"Nineteen." Pete replied.

"Why would someone your age ride his bicycle on these streets just to shovel my drive?"

A little taken-a-back, Pete replied, "My Dad said he will let me get a motorcycle if I pay for it." Pete replied.

"Money . . . the root of all evil. Where are you going to ride it? You can't ride it on the street." Pete heard the voice of Santa from A Christmas Story tell Ralphie, "You'll shoot your eye out kid."

"My Mom and Dad say that, too!" Pete replied.

Ms. Strickland giggled, paused for a moment, and then said, "Well if my son wanted a motorbike, I'd tell him the same thing and hope that he'd give up so I wouldn't have to let him waste his money on a stupid motorcycle."

"They say it's a waste of money, too." Pete said.

"Well, I think its good you have a goal. Now you just need to stick to it and see it through to attainment. How much have you saved so far?"

Afraid she would mock Pete, he reluctantly replied, "Two hundred seventy-five."

"And how much do you need?" She queried.

"Five fifty." Pete uttered.

"Just barely halfway there." Margaret said, and that comment put things into perspective for Pete. He was calculating how many drives he shoveled and how many more it would take to reach $550. Excluding today, it would take twenty-five drives if he shoveled with Mel, and ten if he shoveled himself.

She must have noticed and said, "You're doing the math, aren't you?"

Pete nodded.

She said, "Two hundred seventy-five dollars is a good chunk of change. Someone your age could do some real damage at the comic book store."

"Comics are for kids." Pete thought to himself.

"You know, ladies like money too. Does your little girlfriend know you're such a high-roller?" She giggled.

Pete was offended and she could tell. She went on, "Oh relax. I'm just busting your chops. You're probably too old to like comics but too young to be interested in girls. The point is save your money! Even though you aren't yet at the halfway point, don't get discouraged and give up. Two hundred dollars is probably the most money you've ever had in your lifetime and believe me, it spends easier than it's earned! Each time you spend, you increase the distance to your goal, so don't waste it! Speaking of goals, which house is yours?"

"Fifth house on the left." Pete responded.

As they pulled into his drive, she added, "Get your bike while I write you a check."

When he returned to the passenger side door to retrieve his money, she said, "Maybe by the time you earn enough to buy a motorbike, you'll realize that your parents are right. There isn't enough room back there to ride it, but until then, stick to your goal."

The last thing he wanted to hear was an adult's discouraging comments. Being the self-important chap that he was, Pete expected more than the usual rate, because after all, he did essentially shovel "two snows" and he "rode his bicycle on those streets just to shovel her drive." Much to his disappointment, the check was written for the standard $25.

Before he had a chance to voice his concern, she yelled out, "Shut the door. Its cold! See you next snow!" That was the last snow for the season—which was good because Dustin didn't bring the snow blower back.

Ms. Strickland was right. It was very tempting to spend the money on a new remote control car or other frivolous things—especially since he still had a lot to earn and no good way of doing it or speeding up the process. When it warmed up and the grass began to grow, Pete mowed his own lawn each week. Although he liked the consistent revenue earned from mowing the lawn, he did not enjoy it, and despised the weekly burden. The realtor of the empty house next door even asked Pete if he would be interested in mowing that yard as well. Although it would bring him closer to his goal, Pete didn't want the obligation. As it was, he dreaded his parents suggesting he get up early to cut the lawn before it gets hot or remind him there is rain in the forecast. Pete didn't like being told what to do, especially since they were right. The east coast produced a steady, consistent rains . . . sometimes for a week. He missed a week because he didn't heed his Dad's warning to mow the day before the rain began. Pete's stubbornness forced him to learn things the hard way. The next week it took three times as long to mow since he was cutting two weeks worth of growth stimulated by all the rain—forcing him to empty the bag more frequently.

The anticipation

Once the grass stopped growing for the season, Pete was still short forty dollars. He knew his Dad would not let him borrow the money and Pete was too proud to ask. Until the next snow fall, the only source of revenue was raking leaves. Being so close to his goal, Pete could just smell the unburned gas fumes in the air. Maybe he was huffing it because he finally decided to rake the leaves in his yard and his neighbor's to put him over the edge.

He practically ripped the check from the realtor's hand and ran full sprint home to count his loot. Just to make sure. Once the check was cashed, he'd have $560. It was just barely enough to buy the motorcycle, a gas can, and fill it with gas. Pete would have to wait until the following Saturday to make the purchase since his father insisted on witnessing the sale and he was leaving

Sunday for a week-long business trip. It was the longest week Pete could ever remember, probably for his mother, too. Pete kept bugging her to take him to K-Mart so he could buy the gas can and fill it with gas to be ready to ride Saturday. She came up with some inventive stall tactics, but finally the "don't make me tell your father" threat silenced him.

The purchase

Finally the purchase day came. The funny thing was, Pete had never ridden a motorcycle until that day, not even the one he worked so hard to buy. Would he even like it? Would he be able to ride it? Hell of a time to find out! He understood the "clutch" concept but had heard horror stories of "popping the clutch" and people being thrown off the back. Because of this fear, he stalled it a few times before he was able to get going. When he did, he went racing up the hill, switching gears and using the clutch without a problem. He turned around and coasted into the drive. Speed tears filled his eyes from the cool wind. He let go of the clutch, essentially "popping it" to wipe his eyes and the bike jerked forward, startling Pete, and killing the engine.

His Dad said, "Kill the engine, then let the clutch out."

Pete's friend and the bike's owner laughed.

Embarrassed and afraid his Dad might change his mind because Pete didn't know what he was doing, he tried to cover it up by saying, "I know, I know. Where's the off switch?"

In unison, all three, including his Dad (who had never ridden a motorcycle in his life) said, "by your thumb!" again, followed by laughter.

At that point, his Dad said, "So how much for the machine?"

The owner replied, "$550 with a helmet."

For a minute, Pete thought his Father was going to negotiate a lower price for him, but instead heard him ask, "Do you have the title?"

Pete's stomach sank. Title? What the heck is that? I already know it's a Honda? Pete assumed he meant the owner's manual.

The owner replied, "I don't think you need one?"

Pete could tell this response irritated his Dad immensely and thought for sure he was going to change his mind. Instead in a sarcastic tone, he replied, "Is your Dad around? Maybe you should ask him?"

The owner, who was a year younger than Pete, ran inside to go ask. Pete's Father glanced off to the distance avoiding eye contact with Pete or his friend. Pete could feel the impatience-induced heat radiating from his Father, so he kept his mouth shut and looked at the bike—acting like he knew what he was inspecting. After what seemed like an eternity, the owner came back and said, "My mom said you don't need one."

His dad replied, "How can you not need one?"

The owner replied, "Well, I think she said because it doesn't need a license plate you don't need a title."

Pete's dad sighed and after a moment replied, "What about bill of sale or proof of ownership?"

The owner replied, "We own it."

"I know that," his dad barked, "but what's to show that Pete owns it? If he still decides to buy it?"

"Hold on." The owner replied and ran back inside.

Pete's dad shook his head and looked at the ground and then quickly shifted his glance up at the sky mumbling something. A few minutes later the owner came back and said, "My Mom said she'll type a receipt at work Monday."

Pete was almost sick with anticipation. Finally Pete's Dad gave him his disapproving and somewhat disappointed look and said, "It's your money, Pete. But if I catch you riding it on the street or on the lawn, it's coming straight back here!" He turned and walked towards the car.

Pete interpreted that as final "approval," but reluctantly stuttered, "So I can get it?"

His Dad shouted, "Yes! But walk it home on the street."

He got in the car, slammed the door, and sped off. Ms. Strickland came to mind when she said, "Well if my son wanted a motorbike, I'd tell him the same thing and hope that he'd give up so I wouldn't have to let him waste his money on a stupid motorcycle."

For a split second, Pete contemplated not buying it, but being the stubborn soul that he was, reluctant to take advice from adults—especially his parents—Pete bought the motorcycle.

The end

As with Ralphie getting hit in the cheek not far from his eye with a ricocheted BB, Pete quickly learned that doubting adults and even his own parents were right. There really wasn't enough room to ride it in the woods and he quickly became bored. Like Ralphie, Pete kept this foible to himself. Instead, Pete rode the dirt-bike on the asphalt driveway and tried to master the "wheelie."

Most importantly, Pete achieved his goal.

Epilogue

As luck would have it, a few months after Pete made the purchase, his father took a position out of state and strongly urged Pete to sell the motorcycle immediately, which he did. Again, instead of taking his parents advice and saving the money for a real car, Pete bought a 1/8th scale gas powered radio control car kit, the Kyosho "Integra 4WD Vanning."

His father started the new job and was only home on the weekends, so Pete built the chain driven 4 wheel drive, buggy on his own. Being early spring, there were no drives to shovel or lawns to mow yet, and it seemed like he was ordering parts or begging his Mom to make trips to the hobby store every couple of days because he broke something out of haste. The true cost of negligence finally hit home when he didn't have the money for a part necessary to finish the build and finally run the car until he mowed the lawn . . . next week.

When Pete got the buggy running, he was terrified by its speed and power! It was too small to run in the rocky woods behind his house, but too big for his driveway and it had the tendency to tear up the lawn. The only place it could be safely driven was on the street, so Pete would chase cars with his buggy and drive along side them once he caught up to them. This was all fun and games until the receiver battery went dead with the throttle wide open and the buggy drove into a neighbors planter at 50+ MPH where it knocked over the bird bath and sat throwing freshly planted mulch everywhere with all four wheels.

After the runaway fiasco, the buggy never ran quite the same, and after they moved, it never ran again. Now entering High School, Pete should've taken his parents advice, and saved his money for a real car.

Conclusion

Pete entered the office world several years later, doing what he thought he'd never do, sit at a desk behind a computer. At this first "real job" he noticed several parallels between multimedia projects, their task organization and completion, and shoveling snow.

The big boy shovel, reminded Pete of the conundrum cliche, "Never enough time to do it right, but plenty of time to do it over." In the shoveling context, the shovel pushes the snow until the buildup becomes too difficult to push. The pile then needs to be scooped away and the snow buildup that was pushed over the shovel must be cleaned up. In media, the big boy shovel equates to ignoring seemingly trivial issues until they coalesce into a weighty problem often with interrelated consequences. Had the little issues been resolved upon occurrence, they wouldn't have turned into a big problem.

As much as Pete didn't like splitting the money with Mel, the partnership was beneficial to both, especially Pete. This expanded his potential customer base and he was able to use Mel's tools. The division of labor was mostly equal and they would pickup each other's slack when necessary. In the business world doing such a thing seems to promote complacence.

In business fast, cheap, and good are the goal, but in reality, only two can be achieved. If they want it fast and cheap it won't be good, but if they want it good and cheap it won't be fast. With computers, there is usually some hardware or software that will maintain consistency while increasing output, but it's rarely cheap. If you write/build/roll your own, it may be fast and cheap, but quality will suffer or produce unforeseen consequences, like the snowblower and the newspaper.

Getting in the groove and honing the technique of completing a task is always rewarding, especially where efficiency or effectiveness are concerned. Many of the snow shoveling challenges reminded Pete of the saying, "Work smart, not hard." Now sitting behind a desk as a multimedia developer, there seems to a battle between the cliches, "Do you want it fast, cheap, or good? Pick two," and, "work smart, not hard." In the end, his conscience governs his actions by telling him to perform a task with the same attention to detail he would expect if he was paying someone to do the work for him.

About the author

Pete Thompson is one who insists on learning the hard way, his way. Trial and error may not seem productive, but learning from error and applying the experience is. This is Pete's first book which reflects upon his childhood goal, proving to him, the journey is more important than the destination.